Praise for *Between Gone and Everlasting*

"In *Between Gone and Everlasting*, Danita Dodson crafts love songs to counter mourning, to remember and travel old roads, and to recollect mementos both tangible and heartfelt. Quilts fluttering on a line beckon the reader to stand in the present and revisit a world and loved ones now dead and to worship in cathedrals of green, draw strength from the earth, and perhaps receive a trail-side baptism."

—*JANE HICKS*,
author of *The Safety of Small Things*

"Danita Dodson's poems in *Between Gone and Everlasting* touch lovingly on the painful but essential aspects of loss, and they transcend elegantly to the healing strength that emerges from reconciling such losses as natural consequences of living. In this beautifully written book, the reader, like the poet, can revel in nature and step 'light to the water's edge' and 'go in, go under, come up, / a creature restored and made whole.'"

—*ARTHUR J. STEWART*,
author of *The Hallelujah Series and Other Poems*

"Danita Dodson's *Between Gone and Everlasting* is a love song to a past never truly out of reach. The opening poems reveal the speaker's deep grief over the sudden loss of her father but also trace her journey to understanding how memories become 'light in a dark room' and how 'love outflies the edges of life and death.' Ultimately, the scope of Dodson's collection widens to admiration for all her forebears as well as agrarian life too quickly vanishing. These poems are a sensitive reminder that those who have gone before are 'asking that we keep their echoes with us.'"

—*PEGGY HAMMOND*,
author of *The Fifth House Tilts*

"In *Between Gone and Everlasting*, Danita Dodson's voice captures the magic of the ordinary, where 'the real miracle was that I noticed.' These poems celebrate a lifetime of experiences imbued with humor, sorrow, and love that come from insight learned (sometimes too late). Offering a poignant reminder of both the joys and insecurities of growing up and growing old, the poet recognizes loss in all its forms as she honors the truth of 'leaving a signature of what you've lived, / just like trees and rocks leave marks.' This well-crafted collection is one the reader will reach for again and again."

—*KB BALLENTINE*,
author of *Spirit of Wild*

BETWEEN GONE AND EVERLASTING

## ALSO BY DANITA DODSON

Poetry
*Trailing the Azimuth*
*The Medicine Woods*

Nonfiction
*Teachers Teaching Nonviolence*

# Between Gone
# and Everlasting

*Poems*

## DANITA DODSON

RESOURCE *Publications* · Eugene, Oregon

Resource Publications
An Imprint of Wipf and Stock Publishers
199 W. 8th Ave., Suite 3
Eugene, OR 97401

www.wipfandstock.com

PAPERBACK ISBN: 979-8-3852-1309-2
HARDCOVER ISBN: 979-8-3852-1310-8
EBOOK ISBN: 979-8-3852-1311-5

04/29/24

The excerpts from T.S. Eliot's *The Waste Land* are reprinted by permission
of Faber and Faber Limited.

In memory of my father
Alfred Clarence Dodson
1936-2022
*gone but everlasting*

∞

It's not forgetting that heals.
It's remembering.

—AMY GREENE, BLOODROOT

# Contents

*Thanksgivings and Acknowledgements* | xi

**Whippoorwill's Call**

No Trail Through Grief | 3

Cruel April | 4

Dragonfly's Vigil | 6

Stark Shock of Summer | 8

My First Memory of Death | 9

River Rue | 10

Creature Messages | 11

The Heart's Acceptance | 12

Postcard from Paradise | 13

Consolation of the Bard of Amherst | 14

Dichotomy of Loss | 16

Monet Bouquet | 17

Threads | 18

**Photomosaic**

Range of Vision  |  21

Walking Home  |  23

Legacy of Precision  |  25

Photo of Boy in Sheriff Uniform  |  27

The New Corn Ripples  |  29

Revisiting Roads  |  30

Song Leader  |  31

You Kept  |  33

Welfare Worker  |  35

Clarence's Counsels  |  37

Forever Love  |  38

Sisters  |  40

Invincible  |  42

O, Rhododendron Soul  |  43

**Map of Home**

Hiraeth  |  47

Memory Keepers  |  49

Molten Clocks and Undying Hills  |  50

Bits and Pieces  |  52

Observing the Remains  |  54

Heaven as Highway 33  |  56

The Upstairs Rooms  |  57

Quilted Lore  |  59

Appalachian Action Verb  |  60

Airing the Quilts  |  61

Simple Were the Days  |  62

Butterfly Ancestors  |  64

Old Gray Barn | 65

Reason for Summer Preserves | 66


**Light in the Mourning**

Front Porch Meditation | 69

Rising Goodness | 70

A Pew in the Forest | 71

Remembrance | 73

The Nature of a Phoenix | 74

Trusting Silence | 75

Deadwood Life | 76

Sacred Signatures | 77

Meditations in a Study | 78

Momiji Memorial | 79

Driftwood Diva | 81

Psalm of the Grieving Gardener | 82

Trailside Baptism | 83


*Notes* | 85

# Thanksgivings and Acknowledgements

WHILE WALKING THROUGH THE PROCESS of grief after the sudden death of my father, I have often been bemused by the dichotomy of two words, both woven into this collection: *gone* and *everlasting*. *Gone* speaks to the abysmal awareness of the irreversible loss of someone dear. *Everlasting* signifies the persistence of memory, the meditation upon eternity, and the enduring echoes of the departed. On most days, we the bereaved perhaps linger somewhere *between* two poles of being. Between where we mourn the gone and where we celebrate the everlasting, we sit with grief in an umbral space—a threshold where the past merges with the present. It is here that grievers realize another paradox of lamenting the departed: the unalterable absence sheds light upon that which remains. Meditation upon the remnants—experienced vividly through emotions, memories, objects, and places—has stirred me to create the poems in this collection. For the healing power of language, I offer thanksgiving.

With deep gratitude I acknowledge the editors of these publications, where the following poems first appeared, some in a slightly different form:

- *Amethyst Review*: "A Pew in the Forest"
- *Braided Way*: "Remembrance" (formerly published as "Zikr")
- *Heimat Review*: "The Upstairs Rooms" and "Heaven as Highway 33"
- *Jarfly*: "My First Memory of Death" and "Hiraeth"
- *Salvation South:* "Observing the Remains," "Airing the Quilts," and "The New Corn Ripples"
- *Tennessee Voices Anthology, 2022-2023* (Poetry Society of Tennessee): "Appalachian Action Verb"
- *Tennessee Voices Anthology, 2023-2024* (Poetry Society of Tennessee): "O, Rhododendron Soul" and "Bits and Pieces" (Best of Fest prize)

Thanks is uplifted to friends and family who inspired a few of these poems: Matthew Collins for "Heaven as Highway 33," my sister Malisha Seals for "Bits and Pieces" and "Sisters," Rev. Tommy Seal for "Simple Were the Days," and Ellen Jenny England for "Trailside Baptism."

My heartfelt gratitude flows to several dear author-friends for their encouragement and support. Thanks to Rita Sims Quillen for inspiring me to share the spirit of my father in poetry. Thanks to Amy Greene for permission to use a quote from her bestselling novel *Bloodroot* for the book's epigraph. And many thanks to Arthur J. Stewart, Peggy Hammond, Jane Hicks, and KB Ballentine for graciously endorsing this collection.

Thanks to the editorial team at Wipf and Stock Publishers for helping me bring *Between Gone and Everlasting* to life.

I am grateful to Faber and Faber in London for granting me permission to reprint two excerpts from T.S. Eliot's *The Waste Land*: "April is the cruelest month" and "handful of dust."

I send out a very special thanks to my uncle, Earl Lee Dodson, my father's younger brother. During the past two years, he has embraced me as a daughter and has been enthusiastic about my poetry. Also, watching him face terminal leukemia with courage and with grace has taught me so much about living fully each day. Moreover, it has been an inspirational blessing to listen to him share many beautiful memories and stories about the old days.

And finally, because I feel that he can celebrate my gratitude in the everlasting, I want to say, "Thank you, Daddy, for everything." Hopefully, the book itself mirrors the thanksgiving of an adoring daughter.

# Whippoorwill's Call

∞

# NO TRAIL THROUGH GRIEF

A hillwalker on an uncharted journey,
    I must walk where there
      is no trail through grief—
adrift in this dense, craggy wilderness.

No one has given me a map to use,
    and the compass dial cries,
      baffled about the path,
gyring as though an unsounded lodestone

has engulfed all the earth beneath me,
    where the murky soil of dearth
      makes each tread a silent plaint
in an annulus where I'm affixed to loss.

The azimuth is faint and transmuted
    across hours, days, and months—
      causing me to doubt whether
I have trekked miles or just a few steps.

Yet, as there can be no turning back,
    I'll thwack the stygian wilds
      and slumber on a moss floor—
a lost creature near a whippoorwill's call.

# CRUEL APRIL

—after T.S. Eliot's *The Waste Land*

From this day forward,
I feel I'll forever blame
the coming of spring
for your fleet-footed
                    leaving—

a vapor of light and mirth
dissolved in the gloaming.

*April is the cruelest month,*
as the poet warned it was,
reality in a *handful of dust*
left now where dogwoods
                    wait to bloom—

life's florescence forsaken
after I found you
            silent and lifeless
on the earth from which
the dandelions will flower.

And in the days to come
it will be hard to take joy
in green grass
                    and bees.

And in the days to come
            it will hurt to see
the stemmed sunshine
in the celandine poppies

                    leaping
across the slopes
of the awakening ridge
where mockingbirds sing.

# DRAGONFLY'S VIGIL

The dragonfly pirouetted a message
on transparent white wings dotted black,
daedal codes I could not decipher
under the immense burden of sorrow.

Appearing one night after you departed,
it kept a hushed vigil on the ceiling,
like a watchful father fixed in a chair
beside the bed of a feverish child.

And the real miracle was that I noticed,
saw it lingering there the next morning,
an iridescent sentry who conveyed
a sign that you somehow still parent me.

The next evening, it remained on the wall.
Then suddenly, its wingbeats shimmered
like a silver comet across the night sky
of my heart, flying to land at my side.

When it closed its wings as if to bow,
I moved from the chair to bow also—
to face an ethereal dragonfly head-on
and ask a question: *Is that you, Daddy?*

And when it heard me whisper *Daddy*,
the wings opened like outstretched arms,
reaching out with stirring solace to say,
*Love outflies the edges of life and death.*

Absorbing the awe of whispered truths,
I let it linger for a time, then gave it up
to the windowsill and the open darkness,
grateful for the thin place where we meet.

# STARK SHOCK OF SUMMER

After waiting the cold, dark months
for the bare trees to seize life
by the quickened roots and branches,

> suddenly the green besieges,
> like too much of a good promise.

Then soon the slumberous ridge awakes
to leap forth like a mountain lion,

> surprising in its fecund chaos,
> obscuring the earth underneath.

And the garden you did not help me plant
this year is shocked by weeds' onslaught,

> reminding me of the things
> that grow out of our hands,
> that become too large to hold—

> like grief—

the things we cannot pare down or put
into any kind of order, such as memories

> that visit us in the midnight hours
> or love that overspreads the heart.

# MY FIRST MEMORY OF DEATH

was perhaps the morning after
I took the evening's pleasure
of capturing lightning bugs,
forcing shut the lid upon them,
watching their flashing beauty
dance upon my nightstand
'til I fell asleep in their glow—
not understanding at the time
that their temporal light
was meant to be pardoned
from captivity in a Mason jar,
and from my sorrow at finding
them in the early hours of dawn
asleep to rise no more,
their light switches extinguished
in front of a child who once
had felt that all things bright
and beautiful will always last
just because we want them to,
unaware that we have no control
over the span of time we have
with people we love and cherish,
whose candescence stays with us
for a briefer time than we realize,
so we should find moments often
just to sit on the porch with them
under the evening's obsidian sky
and watch their soul lights dance.

# RIVER RUE

It engulfs me like a river flooded,
its fluxes rising at full tilt,
a boon born of love—
                                    this unmooring,
this opening and spilling of vital pain

that tugs at the thread of the universe,
disheveled at times,
                              also stretched to limits,
yet berthed in something everlasting,
the lifeblood and blessing of the All.

So I allow it, this deep and holy hurt,
trusting that sorrow heaves out
its own preserver
                                    to hang onto—
the corded void that ties me to you.

# CREATURE MESSAGES

*You must keep your eyes open,*
my cousin said when I told him
about the creatures my father sent
my way after he crossed over—
those orphic glisters of nature
sprinkled 'round me like fairy dust.

*Several people noticed that day*
*the joyous mockingbird singing*
*at your Daddy's graveside service.*

I recall, too, how it trilled its notes,
so constant, drowning the words
of the preacher's voice and the sobs
gushing from the cave of my soul.

Later, a dragonfly kept watch
over my bed like an attending angel,

a five-lined skink scurried under
the chair where he had always sat,

and a black swallowtail butterfly
fluttered around his red Tacoma
for a whole day, as though it might
drive miles and miles to get to me,

revealing that there's a nearer kinship
'twixt the earthbound and the divine
than the living can ever quite grasp—
and what we might believe to be gone
finds a way to show us it's everlasting.

# THE HEART'S ACCEPTANCE

When the torrents of lament
                immerse you,
kneel deep inside yourself, child,
like the fingers of a worn glove
                turned inwards,
or like the head of a box turtle
bowed low upon its plastron,
knowing it's alright to retreat

because the heart accepts it all
                at these and other times,
receives this groaning of spirit—
the turmoil of feeling displaced,
the fatigue from sleepless nights,
the pain of missing someone so,
the struggle to reach a safe place
that somehow feels like home.

And it gathers you with kindness,
like a mother-bird reaching out
to usher a shivering baby creature
into the fold of its soft wings,
                reuniting you with essence,
returning you to the arms of Being,
the No-place that is Someplace,
where you feel the refuge of love.

## POSTCARD FROM PARADISE

He sent a wordless image soon after
he departed these green-graced mountains
as the sun was setting low—a place he
never would have left unless he had to,
where raspberry skies define the gloaming
and sunrises taste like lemon meringue.

But here is not there—no way to compare
the dazzling new world beyond my vision,
which I've not yet been invited to view
because it's not time for me to go, so
I dream heaven in monochrome for now
but trust that forever looks a bit like here.

# CONSOLATION OF THE BARD OF AMHERST

—after Emily Dickinson

I paid a call on the Bard of Amherst
When I needed the balm of imagery—
This Picture of worded dimensions
Who whispered that *Grief is a Mouse*
As I walked in her upstairs bedroom
While New England's noonday sun
Streamed through the large windows,
Her many Worlds outside framed
As she spoke in the poetics of glass,
Her wind-eye turned upon me, calling
Me to *measure every Grief I meet*
With an intent gaze and the kindness
To wonder *if It weighs like mine*—
Because *The Grieved—are many*—

The Bard is a Tune I have heard too,
Whose cadences rise from a Well,
*Enlightened to a larger Pain*—
Becoming more powerful in sound
As they leave the sepulcher of mind
And drift over the green-graced Trees
As if played upon some Aeolian harp
For somnolent Vagabonds to hear,
From wherever they wander to here,
Stirring as *imperceptibly as Grief*
Into sunny summer days, taking up
Residence in a heart opened by love,
Bringing Hope where Heartache is—

So I bade this Picture and this Tune
To meander my heart and my mind
And greet a wayfarer on her journey
As a kaleidoscope of poetic purpose,
Bounding Space and Time to tell me,
*'Tis good—the looking back on Grief.*
And I fathom that missing its essence
Or ignoring its complex beauty would
Be, in itself, an Affliction and a Loss,
So I *own her for a Friend* and weigh
The measure of her truth with mine,
Which presently *feels so old a pain*—
As I try to face the days with courage,
Trusting that *I can wade Grief* too—

# DICHOTOMY OF LOSS

Ephemeral is the voice of earth,
its quiddity to linger between
the staying and the leaving,
the truth written on the breeze
that will mingle with the soil,
growth and decay concatenated
in the everlasting circle of life
that unfolds beauty from death,
sunning joy into sorrow's rain,
writing grief in wildflowers,
painting peace in thunderclaps.

# MONET BOUQUET

On a snowy day, to your grave I went
that very first Christmas without you,
recalling the way you left us in spring,
so I carried breathing blooms to you—
       even if it was the midst of winter
and I knew they wouldn't survive long.

A poinsettia it was, a "Monet,"
the florist had said smugly as though she
thought it was art, but maybe it was—
       a surreal form of the original,
not the rich, deep-red, velvety kind
but a lemon-hued plant with a pink blaze.

Its waiflike shape hinted time's tenuity,
       a light now beginning to vanish,
like a blush on skin fading fast,
or like bloodstains from a needle-pricked
finger on a linen washed and bleached—
an engrained proof of a once-pulsing life.

Days later, I found Monet wilted,
       dowsed in icy dew and bowed low
as if in a prayer it knew God would grant.
I fancied you'd flown in like a hummingbird
to quaff the last flushes of its glowing life—
and you remembered that I remembered.

# THREADS

Though it undoes the heart in its homeplace
like a seam ripper slitting the familiar threads
of a cherished heirloom quilt always in view,
its once-fastened lines and borders frayed,

      grief still holds onto the patches . . .

refusing to yield the imprinted fabric of years—
such as a daughter's memory, resistant to wear,
of the day you insisted I meet Shakespeare,
giving me a book of the Bard's seamwork,
knowing I would stitch my own life's rhyme.

The taut fibers of gratitude are woven in me,
and memories aren't as gossamer as I thought
they might be, smiling as light in a dark room,
like the shine of the Epiphone's wooden frame
that you placed in my hands for the sake of joy.

Humming a hymn for me in the distance,
you remind me that I have been sewn to you—
old man walking floors in a tatty, gray sweater,
your hands tucked inside its pockets as if you
held onto the very yarns of life knitted there.

These strands now guide me through the maze,
as I follow the path from one remnant to another,
basted like . . . footprints . . . on a calico road,
or a redbird's song in the entwined eternity,
stitching where you've been to where you are.

# Photomosaic

∞

# RANGE OF VISION

Through the broad lens of time,
I focus light upon the artifacts
of your life that I've begun to find
in the basement, barn, and closets,

searching like a plundering pirate
who gleans all ships on the sea,
rummaging in the random rubble
to unearth a life lingering in things,

seeing you as you really were
in these shoes your feet wore,
in these tools your hands guided,
in these papers your heart wrote,

which I'm learning is a reality
that feels much less like losing you
and so much more like finding you
anew, as you once were—here.

Reading a note, holding a ring,
recalling a song you used to sing,
I am looking at you in time's prism,
as through a glass kaleidoscope,

where I am inspired to turn to learn
how the many reflected pieces of you
dazzle together like a photomosaic
in an aberrated blueprint of your life,

like one of your mother's bold quilts
sewn of the spirit's blue-green ridges,
or like a spiraling dervish dance on
the sunny rug of the universe's soul.

## WALKING HOME

The last walk that Daddy ever took
on this side of life's wide rainbow
was from the barn to the house
after he'd put the tractor to bed
at the end of the long day, caring
more about its rest than his own,
using his feet one final time
to tread that old path he'd carved
around this homeplace he'd built
from the sweat of his brow,
the tools he held in his hands,
and the electric fire of his brain.

So tired he was at the day's end,
placing one foot in front of another
was hard, those Ariat Terrain boots
bearing his aged frame as well as
his last wish to step inside again
and have his supper in the twilight,
sapped from cutting creek-bank trees
to keep a clean line around the farm,
dragging their conquered errant trunks
to a tree-graveyard in the deep woods—
tasks I now feel only a superhero
could accomplish at age eighty-five.

I wish his first workday of spring
had not been overcast and chilly.
I wish his last full day of life
had been sunshiny and temperate.
And I wish he had not just *almost*
made it home, falling short of the door

by a few feet. But he parked himself
behind that old black Ford F-100
like he was petting it one last time
at the close of a good life, as if to say,
*I never was confined to a deathbed.*
*I went by working. I went by walking.*

*And child, I made it home. All the way.*

# LEGACY OF PRECISION

As I look upon who you were,
seen anew through the things
your hands once touched,
which I took for granted before,
like the zoetic trees in the yard
that you planted through the years
in all the right places
        between earth and sky,
I now linger most around

what seems like a memorial
that you built for yourself
in the last year of your life—
an elongated, sarsen rectangle,
a cairn that's turned sideways,
my inheritance of these rocks
rising like a desert memory,
a mirage gleaming in the sun,
a message to the left-behind.

Stones anchored by stones,
each arranged in its new place
        to assert symmetry,
this rock garden edging a house
is a legacy of precision to me—
a dower of the rhyme and reason
that you saw in the universe,
knowing secrets of its numbers
and inherent laws of its gravity.

        And only you could
have had the mathematical mind

to make large stones spill and flow
like an enlivened stream down
the sloping green bank of the yard,
mirroring life's forward force
that ran as well within you—
the something fluid in the solid,
the something eternal ∞ in the finite.

And only you could
have taken each singular rock
in hand and studied it, placing it
just where you knew it belonged,
mindful both of its unique shape
and its connection to others around it,
attentive, too, of the divine plan
of how a life is formed,
of how a family is formed.

# PHOTO OF BOY IN SHERIFF UNIFORM

Seated on the '36 Ford's front fender—
dejected—with hands folded on your lap
      and head bowed, you do not meet
the camera's eye, keeping a solemn watch
over something I cannot see, as you sport
the visor hat and badge of a peacekeeper.

But *you* were only a child back then,
and in my impulse to be a mother to you,
      I would gladly reach my hands out
through the years, through the frame,
through the ancient song of the universe,
just to wipe your tear-stained face.

Perhaps you'd discovered, just before
the lens of life was aimed upon you,
      that being a defender is not so easy.
Other boys notice when your guard is down.
Sidekicks desert you in the heat of battle.
Outlaws lurk and prowl in the woodland.

I'd seen these ghosts of fears arise again
in the vigils you held for my sister and me,
      and in the lessons of good and bad,
and when we hadn't listened well enough,
you shouldered again the selfsame stance
of the long-ago photo's disenchanted hero.

But you still hold watch over me, Daddy,
though you're no longer here in this life,
      and in those times when grief leaps
toward me like an outlaw to steal my peace,

I wield the shield of congruence, knowing
that *you* now see *me* through a cosmic lens.

# THE NEW CORN RIPPLES

like the waves of an ocean
he has never seen,
reflecting light in motion,
its leaves unfurling like sails,
each stalk a vessel moved
by currents under the earth
guiding the graceful sway,

and he, away from his family
and the farm he loves so well,
is trying to be somebody
more than just a child
of poverty and struggle
born in the Great Depression
in an Appalachian holler,

and he can only imagine it
as he can imagine the sea,
which he's reading about
in Shakespeare and Coleridge,
the rustling whispers
of ancient tales sown
in the soil of new possibilities,

as his dormitory window
is flung ajar now to more
than academic buildings,
open to longing and promise,
open to loss and nostalgia,
dreaming of where he's been,
dreaming of where he'll be.

# REVISITING ROADS

I want to revisit roads before I die,
so I'm taking you with me to show you
where my young feet long ago walked
along Big Creek and old Xenophon,
where my roots are affixed to the soil.

This dirt path leads down to the sandbar
on the Clinch where I once planted
my bare feet and my childhood soul
as I watched the shoals rolling white
and the native catfish jumping up high.

And can you just believe that I hiked
over that ridge, through dense woods,
to Central School as a mere young'un,
walking many years, not missing a day,
conquering even the rain and the cold?

This old road in a holler paved the way
to the little log home where I was born,
no longer standing, but I remember it.
A stream right here kept the milk cold,
and an apple orchard grew over there.

What's this? A piece of broken crockery
lying in the earth that was our trash pile
so long ago. Doesn't surprise me that
something of this place remains. Daughter,
keep it as proof that we were once here.

# SONG LEADER

Standing behind the ancient wood lectern
that bore years of his elders' fingerprints,
my father would clear his throat, look up,
smile and announce a hymnal page number,
then intone like a bright, mellifluous bird
who trusted that its Maker guided a flight
of breath where memory is freed into sound
by filled-in fourths and slow portamentos,
connecting and sliding one note to the next,
a carrying power of vowels projected loudly.

As a natural songcatcher, his voice netted
the old-way melodies, remembering
and claiming them still in modern times:
the trills, turns, and leaps sung not as written
but as aurally learned by generations
of good hillfolk who hadn't read music,
their embroidered note clusters handed down
like the heirloom seeds stored in their cellars,
to be saved and used over and over again—
the nuclei of life, of love, of kinship.

The nasality of his grace notes sounded
like those of his father, and his father before,
recollecting a time much further back when
there were no songbooks in weather-worn
worship houses that'd been as thin and poor
as the folks gathered there, who saw
themselves as heirs of an ancient and sacred
vocal art, so the songs had been lined out,
sung a cappella, just the voices alone
in community uplifting praise to God.

He led his flock to feel that death was
only a dream, that life continued in a land
where roses never fade. He heartened them
about crossing rivers, walking dark valleys,
climbing just another hill—the Appalachian
landscape mirrored in the high-pitched quavers
of a soul's search for grace in a fallen world,
piloted by a voice that was as down to earth
as if he'd dug it out of the mountain itself,
the tones shivering like shouts in his throat.

## YOU KEPT

your father's electric shaving set,
his tin-plated Social Security card,
all your mother's sympathy cards
that she received when he passed on—

mirrors that you didn't want to break,
discovered in bedroom dresser drawers
and on basement shelves, an inherited
superstition you honored 'til the end—

abandoned terrapin shells as a gesture
of empathy because you were haunted
as a kid by the memory of human-like
moans after you threw one into the fire—

college math books with odd formulas
written in your hand, a three-sided ruler,
a universal compass set, all for figuring
the divine design at the universe's heart—

sticky notes with page numbers of hymns
you'd led in church any given Sunday,
comments in a bible, worn from reading,
marked by stains from your fingers as well—

a black Ford F-100 that smelt like the farm,
a cowboy's horse for four decades, though
its frame was rusted, and it was a bit unsafe,
driven your last day to Clonce's Market—

photos of all the happy days with Mama,
her Wind Song perfume and rouge compact,
drawings created by your grandchildren
and given to you with the greatest love—

so many other things that mark the trail
of a life of memories that you counted as
worthy, bearing sounds heavier than words
that speak in the silence without you here—

# WELFARE WORKER

In the early days he followed their steep
tracks up the Ridge and into the hollers
and walked across creaky swinging bridges,
his briefcase in hand, to reach houses built
of flimsy wood, which had cracks so wide
       the snow blew through in the winter.

So he knew how they lived—he had seen it,
noted it all because that was his job,
no longer resolved to become an engineer,
leaving his employ as a math teacher,
called to public assistance, to serve those
       who Jesus said were *the least of these.*

Later, he had to maintain an office,
where one by one they sat before his desk,
the people from up on the highest peak,
those the townsfolk called the *Ridgeminites,*
with cruelty, distaste, and prejudice, but
       he was determined to love them.

Seeing them, he knew their innate goodness,
which the world didn't want to recognize,
and he distributed food stamps to them
as sincerely as one of the disciples
called by Jesus to help make miracles
       from a few bits of fish and bread.

It was his own childhood that rose again
when he saw their struggle and remembered
his life in a holler along Big Creek,
born at history's crux amid two world wars

and the Great Depression in '36
          to sharecroppers fighting to subsist,

who somehow nursed him through scarlet fever,
then rejoiced his healing by insisting
that he walk over two ridges to school,
accepting the help of neighbors who cared—
so he knew well the force of some kindness,
          repaying God's grace to those he served.

# CLARENCE'S COUNSELS

Don't run more water than you need.
Keep your shoes 'til they're worn out.
Or if you see someone who needs them
more than you do, give them away.

Phone me the minute that you get there.
Be cautious of the strangers you meet—
be kind, but don't trust them outright.
Knowing someone well takes much time.

A thing does not happen simply because
we have anything much to do with it.
If the good Lord wills, it will. So always
believe that Something Larger guides you.

Go to church each time the doors are open,
and offer your heart in community there.
Practice a song before you rise to sing it,
knowing its curves, tones, and blessings.

Keep the peace with everyone, even if
you don't agree with what they say or do.
Never raise your voice in anger—being
a peacemaker is the Lord's greatest calling.

When you have enjoyed a wonderful day
and do something beautiful that brings
your heart light, say out loud, *This is living!*
Time is short—and we'll all travel on soon.

# FOREVER LOVE

Daddy was always so sweet on Mama,
their history unearthed the day I found
62 love letters that she had kept,
tied by a golden cord and placed with care
in a keepsake box, records of a love
in its first budding days. *Be cute and be
my girl for always.* He had wanted that.

Then I recalled a family legend
about the quest to find a bright diamond.
Too poor to afford the best, he walked down
Knoxville's busy Gay Street to an alley
stairway leading to a black market "store,"
buying a shimmering ring for the gal
he promised to love *'til death do them part.*

But this would be sooner than he had hoped
when his 60-year-old darling was ravaged
with breast cancer, so he became a soldier
who fought the dark battle alongside her,
doing housework he'd never done before,
asking her to write down her recipes,
staying cheerful and steady in her presence.

And he prayed, *Lord, have mercy on her,*
as he watched her body grow much frailer,
the woman with a spitfire nature who
had always gone full force into the days—
she was sun and rain, and all things honest,
caring for her caretaker, her watchful eye
cast upon him who was standing by her,

finding the strength to piece him a new quilt
as a last love letter to her man, her way
of telling him she would always be near
though her residence would be in heaven.
And over the next nineteen years, she was
there amid the grief and amid life's joys,
writing the truth that love never departs.

## SISTERS

Weaving our imaginations together,
despite the occasional scuffles—
two little balls of curiosity
bright in a house with a weak antenna
and a black-and-white TV—
we were taught to seek our own ways
to create the world and each other.

In winter we formed a society of dolls
and stuffed animals, sheltering them
under quilts thrown over kitchen chairs,
a campsite of imagination,
seating them on stairs to watch games,
placing them in rows to ride buses—
always aware of motion and community.

While the TV soaked up Watergate,
outside we were a summer reality show,
racing across the hood of Daddy's car,
dissecting bugs on a card table in the yard,
leading our dog Junior to chase the light
we bounced off a mirror into the noon sun—
our mayhem fueled by reading and marvel.

We rode doodles on a tricycle's back,
threw cats up in the air like frisbees,
hurled rocks into our teenage neighbor's car
as he sped by on Twin Pines Road,
and on rainy days we stifled our giggles
when the eight-party phone line aired talks
that were not exactly G-rated.

With our creaking bones and graying hair,
now we don't take those days for granted—
memories that are testaments to the parents
who allowed us to find joy in togetherness,
who always taught us that we were equal
portions of a life they had joined together,
linked by a love that would outlast them.

# INVINCIBLE

Dearest daughters of mine, please accept
these last words I never got to tell you—
read them as a letter winged from above,
couriered on the gloaming's sinking sun
as I make my way fast to my new life
in the vast, bright homeland of infinity.
　　　*But I love you still.*

If I had the chance to go back in time
and change anything, I know I would not
because the kind afterlife now tells me
that I was gifted with sufficient grace—
after all, 85.7 x 365 equals
a multitude of beautiful, long days.
　　　*Yet I love you still.*

In the before-life, I felt this when God
breathed to me in the quiet space of prayer,
but not until now do I fully grasp
the ways in which the years planted me
invincible, like a many-ringed tree
still standing when all the world is on fire.
　　　*So I love you still.*

As you look at my face in the coffin,
see the new life that is embering there,
and know wrinkles are roads I'm walking,
each gray hair the song of an enduring man
who will never be altered by time.
For I am not gone. I am everlasting.
　　　*And I love you still.*

# O, RHODODENDRON SOUL

The understory abides in the shade
behind the bright limelight of wonder,
the veiled comrade of the old growth,
obscure green below the overstory,
like the rhododendrons that shelter
underneath impressive tall hemlocks,
fair Robins to the woodland Batmen,
in symbiotic link and tandem life.

Just like them, sweet old gentle man,
you were here in the Appalachian hills,
quietly aiding the largeness of others,
living with them in calm coexistence,
growing miracles even in an acrid soil
that had lost gratitude for men like you—
the ground cover of the old civility,
the underwood of howdies and amens.

A benefactor of unannounced charity,
you helped nurture a whole community,
allowing fresh humble saplings to rise,
looping tangles like arms around those
in your care, nurturing a sense of home
from a single burl of wood, showing how
one rooted individual in life's understory
can grow others upward into the light.

# Map of Home

∞

# HIRAETH

I roll this Welsh word on my tongue,
hear its "r" undulate like a zephyr
afloat in autumnal trees on the ridge,
and I sense a meaning beyond sounds,
its untranslatable depth speaking to me
about this homesickness I feel inside,
dumbfounded with my mouth agape
as an echo rises from somewhere deep.

And I hold it to my heart like a blanket
as if it were a word that's mine to keep,
though I know very well that it is not,
though its resonance brings me comfort.
But it's larger than all our lives here—
we who have ever loved a person,
we who have ever loved a way of life,
we who have ever loved a homeplace.

It's a bittersweet memory of something
now gone, something irretrievably lost,
the longing for a time no longer here,
a home that can never be recreated,
one to which you can never quite return,
even if you have all the old photographs
of how everything was placed in a room,
even if their fingerprints are on the walls.

It's the music you hear inside your head
that you hope you never—ever—forget,
the nostalgia for those who are long gone,
some you never met, but you *know* them,
so you grieve for lost places of the past,

holding memory's long trace of homelands,
the people of one's own blood and family,
and the old traditions and the lifeways.

It's the distinct feeling of missing that
makes the *now* not the same as the *before*,
a lonesomeness both sorrowful and joyful
that springs up thanks for a cherished past
and for those who underwrote who you are,
the resonance of their steps on floorboards,
the clinking of their coffee cups on a table,
the echoes of their laughter still in a room.

# MEMORY KEEPERS

We preserve the cherished keepsakes,
where yesterday wakes and whispers.
We are the guardians of memories,
the attendants of the ancestral flame.
We are gatekeepers who open doors
to let history walk into the now.

We sift through the faded photographs
and recall faces we've never seen.
We cradle the quilts that they made us
from cloth stitched by a story's thread.
We walk the green land they once tilled
and wildcraft the earth's healing herbs.

We're buttons in a King Albert tin,
tea-stained muslins in a cedar chest,
brown calligraphic curves in a bible,
chipped plates and bent forks in a trunk,
timepieces and wedding rings in a box,
bygone songs rising from out of the blue.

We rattle and shake the nails and bolts
stored in the old glass mayonnaise jars,
and we brandish the hammers and saws,
believing that their owners once knew
ways to put closed doors on heartaches
and opened windows on the soul's joys.

# MOLTEN CLOCKS AND UNDYING HILLS

—after Salvador Dalí's *The Persistence of Memory*

I traipse through this fallow wasteland
of weedgrown fields and tumbledown barns,
where ants crawl over the rotting wood
at the ground-walls of the old homeplace—
fragments disjointed into surreal forms,
as time surrenders its once-steady pace.

Hourglass sands never again flow through
my grandfather's treasured timepieces,
now all molten clocks scattered among us,
placed in cedar chests where they wilt
underneath the blues, yellows, and browns
of worn quilts telling of cabins and stars.

Like buzzing insects, time flies swiftly,
collapsing notions of a fixed cosmos
once hinged upon the wholesome comfort
of warm gingerbread from Mamaw's oven,
countless stars in a towerless skyline,
and Papaw's fit hands working miracles.

But memories escape death in these hills,
where the soil honors bloodroot and oaks—
eternal place that my father used to climb
daily as a boy to find the milk cow
and to ponder the poetry in his heart,
a masterpiece of life formed in the hush.

In this canvas of wistful dreams, I walk
as I hear the ancient forest hymns rise
where the old hill-heritage will not die,
even though the oldest hemlock molders.
My footsteps on the wild earth measure
memorial imprints on once-beaten paths.

I will not be one to dismiss the ancestors—
to leave them behind as alien spirits who
others can't seem to identify as their own
in these days of postmodern lostness—
so I will see them in the rooted mountains,
declaring they will have permanence too.

# BITS AND PIECES

In time's wide tapestry, we are woven
threads of history coded, stories stored,

bits and pieces of our ancestors, their
muted secrets embedded in our bones,

ribbons and strands of DNA laced
through our heartbeats and our blood,

breaths that resonate a chorus of lives,
voices of lineage entwined in a chord,

mosaics of gravestones set into place,
marking geography, culture, and race,

branches waving in the wind, willing us
to see their leaved lives in our arteries,

heirs of countless victories and defeats
imprinted immutably in our cells,

kaleidoscopes of features and dictions
turning around the shapes of memories—

like the way I see the past's reflections
surface in the glimmering green eyes

handed down to me from my Daddy,
who inherited his own from his Mama,

those Barnard eyes that look like forests,
which spot afar off the isle of England,

and gazing back at them, whoever they
were, is like looking at a map of home.

## OBSERVING THE REMAINS

In front of a weathered clapboard house,
four bearded irises stand in a row,
like a family posed for a photo,
not bothering this spring to tack up
the faded heirloom quilt behind them
in this place now made of stillness.

The windows sit sigogglin, not plumb
with the planes of rough-hewn lumber.
The chimney of mountain rocks gaumed
with clay is a shambolic song of stone.
The white paint flakes away to expose
the gray moods of immemorial wood.

But this old house is a living presence,
like a granny who catches rainwater
in a barrel to store what's worth saving,
standing as a beacon of memory
near a once-trodden footpath that leads
to a graveyard of castoff objects—

tarnished tin cans and old wheel spokes,
riddled wash pans and riven pots,
worn shoe soles and rusty bed springs,
busted crocks and Ball Mason jars—
all once used in life's fluid motion,
lying now in the green ferns and the hush.

Seeing them here is funereally sad,
like standing over the dead once more,
the remains both gone and everlasting,
vacant footsteps in a clapboard house,

vestiges of a past departing our hills,
asking that we keep their echoes with us.

# HEAVEN AS HIGHWAY 33

Memory is a ribbon of road that rolls
southward from the Clinch River Market,
parallel to the water's flow, buoyant
like a windblown gray rug that drifts
by Camp's Corner and past Swan Creek,
onward to the Claiborne County line,
each mile a waymark of good old days.

This thread of East Tennessee highway
once strung together the homes of the folks
who made this rural community what it was,
those who went to the front porch after supper
to redeem the time and watch who passed,
waving to us young'uns with friendly hands,
sharing smiles that said more than words.

Without them this asphalt artery seems
now just a road, though sometimes I hear
the spirits of their laughter ring the hills,
manifesting the old lessons and the old songs
that tied the porches to fields and churches
as they broke the bread of shared experience
and poured out grace with the sweet tea.

Sometimes I fancy that Heaven mirrors
geographically the best parts of Earth,
not a land for strolling on streets of gold,
but a homeplace where I will arrive just
in time to turn down Highway 33
at the Clinch River Bridge and see them all
smiling and waving as I travel by.

# THE UPSTAIRS ROOMS

Two upstairs rooms—one pink, one blue—
once were collages of heirlooms
in a home where love grew like tall trees,
but now all they contain are quiet ghosts
who once walked the linoleum garden,
where my feet have stepped into daisies
growing out of the first room into the other,
no door between them, only a doorframe
—open—where my father and uncle once
as kids shared freely the heart of their lives
when grace walked these backwoods beams.

A quilt chest sits under a pink sky,
and two black horses gallop on the wall,
heralds above iron-post beds moved from
the family's first home in the holler.
At the foot of one bed is an old trunk that
my grandfather's grandfather carried out
of Virginia with him to Tennessee.
Mamaw's dresses are in the walk-in closet.
The Victrola brings the Carter Family
here to sing "Keep on the Sunny Side,"
and a pump organ lifts the ceiling in song.

I blink, and the furniture is a mirage,
only a phantom—not here at all,
just a dream a once-little girl recalls.
When the truth sets in, the past has passed,
and the beds, the quilt chest, the trunks all
dissolve into gossamer, claimed years ago
by one family member or another.
As I sit on the dirt-laced linoleum,

talking to mute walls and empty closets,
in wistful acquiescence I thank God that
at least the daisies were the last to go.

# QUILTED LORE

The Appalachian Shahrazads once knew
that quilters and storytellers were sisters,
spinners of hill-lore who made motion
amid the mundane—magical realists
who used new languages to tell old truths,
putting wand-work and quilting needles
on the wisdom cloths of everyday use,
finding purpose in their bereavement,
streaming light into shadowy rooms
to make dolls dance and butterflies flutter.

Those quilting grandmothers once sewed
shivering tales of spirits that hover
still in the mist of the mountains with us—
graveyard rumblings, headless horsemen,
haunted cabins, witches on the hilltops.
They recited them with a prickling skill
that made us believe the mountains take on
an undying life of their very own,
persisting so much longer than we will
ever possibly be able to grasp.

Erstwhile awing us with enchanting tales—
we kids who had no TikTok or Disney—
the lore-stitchers withdrew without notice,
leaving us spellbound Aladdins afloat
in suspense on cheerfully pieced patchwork,
making us find our way home from distant
worlds that still seemed *here*, jolting us back
into our routine rural realities,
saying, *That's jist whut they said happened.*
*I don't know if hit's the truth or not.*

# APPALACHIAN ACTION VERB

*Cobble*—as a verb,
from Middle English "coblen,"
now chiefly Southern Appalachian, meaning
to mend or patch coarsely,
to make do with almost nothing,
to slap together materials hastily to cover up
      threadbare cracks or denim holes,
to stitch rag calico randomly into a quilt,
to piece together the diverse resonances
      of Scotch-Irish and Cherokee,
      of Melungeon and Affrilachian,
      of bluegrass and fandango,
to cut up and put scraps of dough into cooked fruit,
      preferably blackberries,
to create a jagged trail, a dreamer's path
      into the howling wilderness,
      chopping wild ivy and thorn to see daylight,
to repair worn soles that have traversed ridges,
to restore the hollows
      caused by hunger, fever, and sorrow,
to heal the earth that has been torn
      by erosion and floods,
      by fracking and mountaintop removal,
to create a plan of activism for fixin' our woes

# AIRING THE QUILTS

In hushed hills where time was stitched slowly,
when the warmth of spring unfurled its embrace
and our yards awoke with the bees' soft hum,

we took them off the beds and into the sun—
our mountain ritual of coming clean,
telling the whole truth about who we were,

showing all the world that we had survived
a cold winter blowing through the cracks
of a run-down place we'd still seen as grace.

On our backyard clotheslines, they fluttered
like multicolored prayers lifted skyward
on the mountain breeze in creation's dance,

and we saw that they were not quite perfect,
mended and resewn through many long years
by hands that threaded lives into the scraps,

each one a kaleidoscope and an ode
to mothers and daughters and grandmothers
who labored to hand down life's patterns.

For this spring rite was as everlasting
to us as the return of green to the hills,
renewing all that would wave as emblems,

all that would never be gone or misplaced
because we'd kept it close to us each day,
airing the truth that it—and we—mattered.

## SIMPLE WERE THE DAYS

when red was read
in the bloodroot and mountain strawberries,
which no one remembers how to find here
anymore, their feet not having touched
the footpaths up the hillside now teeming
with vines and overtaken by brambles—

when we flopped down
on the open tailgate of an old pickup truck,
our Converse sneakers dragging the bottom
of asphalt as we hitched a ride to the store
to spend the money earned topping *'baccer*
on a MoonPie and a cold orange Nehi—

when we stayed *a-wake*
with our recent dead overnight in church,
as their souls finally made the crossing
on home, our hymns floating out of the open
summer *winders* where lightning bugs danced
and whippoorwills sang to consecrate a life—

when the plow broke
the land that we knew well enough to talk
about on front porches with our neighbors,
valuing togetherness and unity, leaning on
each other in a quilted community because
discord and chaos were against our beliefs—

when we listened to trees,
talked to bees, asked daisies in the field
to tell us all the plain truths about love,
running barefoot across mountain ridges,

returning home with berry-stained fingers,
full of the good things we found each day.

## BUTTERFLY ANCESTORS

Sometimes I wonder if butterflies might be the lingering ghosts of the mountain elderly, souls indelibly attached to the soil and the wildflowers, to the signs of the moon and the changing of seasons—symbols of a way of life that is being annihilated by machines and time, and by the sadder tragedy of forgetfulness. But their transformation stories from the cocoons of life's labor, like those my Daddy once told me, speak volumes to us about constancy and courage. In their caterpillar corpses, they felt everything, as they inched their way across the earth that they nurtured and loved each day. Not satisfied with blazing a straight course with perfect angles through the wilderness and just be done with that, they learned how to follow the earth's shape, leaving—allowing—uneven edges while making lateral turns with the plow, following the land's rhythm through the seasons as they coaxed life out of the ground, boding well their time here as they earned wings. Maybe—just maybe—these bright souls reappear to sanctify our day, and we never even know it, except when sometimes we smell the sweet scent of flowers and hear the soft fluttering of wings coming to light upon our memories.

## OLD GRAY BARN

Old gray barn—the field's aged sentinel—
time has etched its mark upon your frame,
just as it's left age spots upon my own,
both of us in view of a world speeding by.

In your glory days you were a stormproof,
nut-brown source of pride for your farmer,
who once looked upon you as a lighthouse
through seasons of bloom and waning light.

Then such a thing was built to last, sturdy
as the chestnut before the blight of his kin,
years ago when the woods were much more
alive than we can now possibly know.

Though your boards groan like elderly bones,
you stand near the green corn, absorbing it
like a lifeline while folks hightail it past
or misread your abiding presence here.

# REASON FOR SUMMER PRESERVES

After the blisses of dogwoods and apples,
we *d'rectly* bury the spring and the summer,
reshaping the new notes into old tunes,
merging bittersweet pace and lilting truths
as we watch with awe while our landscape
again bleeds, corrodes, returns to its Maker.

And we know it for what it is—this place
where hill people have had to scratch out
a way of life in deep *hollers* of being,
where the old Celtic yearning moves us
toward homesickness for all we have lost,
ancestral memory distilled in us.

But God has shown us how to preserve it,
how to pass down the secret to keeping
ourselves as if we were the sweet berry jam
that we'll open in the winter's murkiness,
as we spoon out the purple hills of summer
and relish the light gathered in our hearts.

# Light in the Mourning

∞

# FRONT PORCH MEDITATION

Only here, perched on my front porch,
can I attend the sounds that mark
my place on the mountain this moment
before sunset, where my neighbor's cattle
bellow in the field straight in front of me,
joining the tunes of mockingbirds,
and this gloaming doesn't feel as lonely
as it once did, and I know that I am—
someday soon, surely—about to step one
toe over the line into a hallowing beauty
that will cleanse me like mountain water
flowing from a cool stream, weaving
stitches of the night into the dawning,
like dark threads sewn onto an old quilt
that was pieced of sunbright patches,
the needle pricking an outstretched hand,
opened to allow hurt into the creation,
holding space to feel love's everything,
so I'm learning to sit as still as a bird
on the porch and listen to the hill-song.

## RISING GOODNESS

Benevolence
arrives like a refulgent dawn,
rolling through my window
to open with quiet promise
the sepulcher that night sealed,
as it eases the certainty of loss
in the waking hour's light.

Kind as a smile
and as unobtrusive as breath,
it carries me forward even
when I feel I cannot reach it,
embracing me like a mother
who's there after her child fell
on the playground—hurt.

Benevolence
assuages sorrow's adamance
with softness of butterfly wings,
and though I do not wake today
seeking this mercy, it flies to me—
regardless—alighting here,
sweet as grace, lingering a while.

## A PEW IN THE FOREST

High on a mountaintop where few ever go,
the autumnal forest rises in splendor
like a cathedral accepting all kinds of seekers
inside its ancient pillars of trees pointed
heavenward. And in a small nave of arched
branches, I listen to the bird-choristers.

The woodland incense of acorn drifts
above the crunch of leaves, both whispered
like prayers for the transcendence of being,
and I know without a doubt something holy
is afloat and afoot in this ephemeral space
that will not look quite the same tomorrow.

But today, sunlight on stained-glass leaves
pulses a reminder of the deep red lifeblood
flowing through the roots of the Spirit,
linking me to all creatures, revealing also
the golden tone of gratitude that is fused
to the breath of the earth if we notice it.

I hear the numinous wood-laced hymns
rebound the flamboyant flutter of a truth,
which I know I must accept here, even as I
pine for the one who has departed from me—
the truth that each of us must pass through
the autumn before living forever in spring.

As a pilgrim humbled by a need to wonder,
I take my pew—this moss-covered log—
sheltered beneath an old oak that's become
my friend, and I embrace the communion,

knowing deeply, even in loss and sorrow,
that God is here, and it is well with my soul.

## REMEMBRANCE

*—on the first anniversary of my father's passing*

One year later, I recall your presence here,
speaking all your names, now divine to me—
Father, Friend, Teacher, Hero, Everything—
recalling too the Being that binds us always
between here and there, where I can sense
the eternal life that I cannot yet see or touch.

So I sing a hymn of praise with a holy *bendir*
in my hand, this music with mystical rhythm
that transcends earthly boundaries as I spiral
through the heart's corridors in celebration,
remembering your soul as a living mandala,
a sacred geometry orbiting the center of life,

unfolding myself like a cosmic lotus that
acknowledges the sun and the rain upon it,
seeking to rise from loss with something new,
something gained that's woven from love—
the harmony in chaos, the peace in turmoil,
and the fixedness in a meandering journey.

# THE NATURE OF A PHOENIX

Morning sings with sunlight on mist,
chaunting consolation for our sorrows,
humming resurrection praise in dew—

a melody for the disappearance of night,
a tune for beginning from ashes anew,
an orb of sweet light glowing like a halo

around this phoenix bird who is an heir
of the blessedness of an old bird's wings,
arisen with gratitude in blue mountains

to engage in wonder about exactly why
so many things of this earth have vanished
while so many more seem unending,

like the sacred hemlocks still standing
that were here before grandparents were,
obelisks of bark rising like memorials

that spawn faith from a pinecone fallen
to earth to resurrect as seeds on the wind,
leaving something behind to regenerate

itself even in a long blaze of mourning,
to raise its wings again in a burst of light,
praising things both gone and everlasting.

## TRUSTING SILENCE

The holy quietness boasts
more sonorous depth
than the finite boom
of a world thrumming fast,
       so as I lean now
into the velvet darkness
of a noiseless reprieve,
I can hear the descant—
the soft song of peace
resounding, its buoyant
rhythmic smile bearing
grace, and the new day
holds much that faith
       must trust—
an eternal joy with light
outlasting the going away.

# DEADWOOD LIFE

The bones of the forest lie wooden,
ostensibly estranged from life,
their arboreal forms descending back
into the earth from which they grew,
forgotten when they fell athwart,
or disdained as dross in a lush grove
because they remind us of death.

But they have more to do with living
than we can ever perhaps imagine
because they refuse to give up Being
even when their roots are pulled out
from under them, their lifelines felled.

With limbs spread supine like a book,
open to read, fallen trees don't pretend
to wither away beneath the moss
that covers them like a green blanket,
for they still support others' aliveness,
a memory bank of cells that will give
inheritance to creatures of all kinds,

reminding us of the hardwood roots
lying solidly beneath our sorrows,
remnants of life that won't be vanished
but will find ways to tell so many stories
in alive things like redbuds and redbirds.

# SACRED SIGNATURES

Little one, read the sacred signatures
written in the roots of the ancient soil
in the blue-green altar of mountains
that lie open like a book of testaments
to your ancestors' footsteps, imprinted
prayers alive in the heart of the land.

Your great-grandpa once walked here—
he whose name rings like a bell in yours,
he who knew the earth's energy binds
all things together like a codex of pages,
forever and always, now and then,

gathering the songs of trees that remember,
absorbing the words of rocks that recall,
each one a chronicle to the old truth:

at birth, you are called to enter a room
through one door, stay awhile and receive
wisdom from all you meet, and then exit
through another door, pouring this light
back into the universe when you depart,

leaving a signature of what you've lived
just like trees and rocks leave marks,
just like spirits of loved ones before you
have always left some residuum
of themselves upon a place like this one,

their life force and prayers ever present,
swirling still like particles all around you
in a dance of light, weaving and blessing
the holy bond between earth and heaven.

# MEDITATIONS IN A STUDY

Sacred space, secret place, shelter
world to create, an altar to pray
to the Spirit who remembers first
the cherubim of a fat-faced infant
with a headful of dark, curly hair,
five months old, laughing at life—
now trapped in a porcelain frame
on a shelf of Appalachian fiction.

Somewhere that smiling baby still
is within me, is alive and innocent
of the truth that parents will die,
that youth will give way to old age,
that change will not change. And
she sits in this room full of books,
gathering the healing truth that
the angels in us can create us anew.

# MOMIJI MEMORIAL

Maybe I'm not as crazy as a bess bug,
but I'm doing what some might think
            is madness anyway—
I'm talking to the Japanese maple,
wishing it to live and thrive,

planted for you a year after your passing
in memory of the way you were rooted
once here in this life, and how you grow
now in a new green garden with Mama.

            I planted it like a prayer.

For abundant blessings—
may samara fruit appear in September,
your birthday month, bearing winged seeds
that will share life on a northwest breeze.

For restorative harmony—
may the tree bring calmness and rest,
celebrating how you created a joyful life,
and enrooting my own peace in the world.

For transforming beauty—
may its elegance hallow my remaining days
as *momiji* turning red with grace in the fall,
reminding me how we all must live seasons.

For poised patience—
because this precarious tree-child of mine
will take a long time to grow and nurture,
like these poems I try to write,

something that keeps me reaching,
imagining that when it's at its final height,
I will be the age you were when you left.

# DRIFTWOOD DIVA

She is like sculpted driftwood—
adaptable and unapologetic,
the architect of her own narrative,
shaped over time by the currents
she has navigated, a chronicle
that isn't over when it washes up
on life's beach, riding the waves
of sorrows or challenges, for she
holds the sands in place and allows
creatures to take root in her shade,
a place of shelter for the abandoned,
the kind refuge of a thousand arms
that embraces all imperfections,
her hair a tangled mess of beauty,
her face smiling in a knurled trunk,
her arms rising upward like mystic
branches to ensign a tree of life
that will never, ever, be finished
because where she goes she will
gather with clusters in the twilight,
and even when it seems there may
come an end to her being, she is
only beginning to sculpt her story.


*—Jekyll Island, September 2022*

# PSALM OF THE GRIEVING GARDENER

*Awake, psaltery and harp—*
it is dawn and time for melody
      after a numb slumber
            in an untilled field,
where I've left the land unseeded
for the fallow time
to allow and honor the grief,
even to speak its name with intent.

But *blow upon my garden—*
God-Wind who has embraced
my pain and has replenished me
      after the long days
            and restive nights,
calling me now back to the earth
of my Father with gratitude
for all the beauty once sown here.

Awake, my soul, and sing aloud—
seasoned by the return of the sun,
chord to every cord that weaves
into the mourning sky, and I will
            tend to the soil,
      tend to the soul,
for a well-watered garden of song
joins the gone to the everlasting.

# TRAILSIDE BAPTISM

River—
from on high You flow,
running holy and clear down
from grace's green throne,
the mountain's birth waters
bursting in expedient rush,
a generous openness of sound
to let us know that life still
abounds in this faraway valley,
where You break us loose
from the dark shadows of death.

Stopped—
in my tracks, I hear You call,
so I pause to listen
to Voice, sensing Presence
here and near, an offering given
to me in this wild, remote space,
as I walk where the sun glitters
like an orbiculate promise
with all the wholeness of joy
that comes after rain settles,
casting light on a purling ribbon.

Familiar—
I embrace You like a child
who knows its mother in its first
few moments of life—following,
meeting, You down in the heart
of the woods, where You pour
Yourself through dirt and trees
like liquid sand in an hourglass,

telling me that time flows too,
so I must also move with rhythm,
sometimes still, sometimes stirring.

Aside—
I lay my backpack full of burdens
and my shoes heavy with life's mud,
removing them—letting them go—
as I tread with care on sacred ground,
down to the sparkling River of God,
down to the current of Your Love,
bare feet touched by nurturing soil,
stepping light to the water's edge—
where I go in, go under, come up,
a creature restored and made whole.

# NOTES

## Cruel April

*April is the cruelest month* and *handful of dust* are quotes from T.S. Eliot's *The Waste Land*. These two excerpts are reprinted by permission of Faber and Faber Limited.

## Consolation of the Bard of Amherst

*Grief is a Mouse, measure every Grief I meet, if It weighs like mine, The Grieved—are many, Enlightened to a larger Pain, imperceptibly as Grief, 'Tis good—the looking back on Grief, own her for a Friend, feels so old a pain,* and *I can wade Grief too* are borrowed from poems by Emily Dickinson.

## Song Leader

The old-way music mentioned in this poem is the traditional style of singing of the Primitive Baptists in Southern Appalachia. In "lined out" music, each line in a hymn's quatrain was first sung by a song leader, followed by the congregation in a melodic repetition of the same words. A "portamento" is a pitch sliding from one note to another. The lines "as down to earth / as if he had dug it out of the mountain itself" are inspired by Appalachian singer Ralph Stanley's remarks about his father: "My father had just an old-time lonesome voice, down to earth like he dug it right out of one of these mountains" (qtd. in Dawidoff, Nicholas. *In the Country of Country: People and Places in American Music*. New York: Pantheon Books, 1997).

## Welfare Worker

The poem quotes the scriptural phrase *the least of these*, which comes from Matthew 25:40 (KJV).

**Molten Clocks and Undying Hills**
This poem is inspired by *The Persistence of Memory*, a painting by the great Salvador Dalí.

**Quilted Lore**
The phrase "everyday use" echoes the title of Alice Walker's short story "Everyday Use."

**Psalm of the Grieving Gardener**
*Awake, psaltery and harp* comes from Psalm 108:2 (KJV), and *"blow upon my garden"* is taken from Song of Solomon 4:16 (KJV).

www.ingramcontent.com/pod-product-compliance
Lightning Source LLC
Chambersburg PA
CBHW060358050426
42449CB00009B/1795